Personal Devotion

K.I.S.S.
Keep It Simple Saints!
-Volume 1 in the Series-

Carlton L. Coon, Sr.

K.I.S.S Keep It Simple Saints - Personal Devotion

© 2020 Carlton L. Coon, Sr.

Scriptures quoted from the King James Version unless otherwise noted.

Published by Carlton L. Coon Sr. Ministries, Springfield, Missouri

Printed in the United States of America

All rights reserved under International Copyright Law

Other Material by Carlton L. Coon Sr.

Carlton and Norma Coon pastor Calvary United Pentecostal Church in Springfield, Missouri. Audio of the preaching and teaching is available at SpringfieldCalvary.church.

Regular blog posts can be received by signing up at CarltonCoonsr.com

Ministry Monday is a short, relevant video provided each Monday on Facebook and as a YouTube channel. Ministry Monday is intended as a benefit to those involved in the "five-fold ministry." *Ministry Monday with Carlton Coon* is also available as a podcast on ITunes and other similar channels.

Disciple-making and Church Growth

Take Root

Take Root Video

Bear Fruit

Bear Fruit Video

Fitly Framed CD

Fitly Framed Video

You Wouldn't Want an Ostrich for Your Mama

How and Why of Hospitality -

How and Why of New Convert Care

How and Why of Follow-up

What the Bible Says (also available in **Spanish**, **French** and **Tagalog**.)

For Preachers

Masterful Preaching

Honey from a Strange Hive

Questions Pentecostal Preachers Ask

Beating the Marriage Busters

Biblical Parenting

The Details Matter: Principles and Practice of Church Administration

Broad Readership

Daily Things of Christian Living

If Everybody Here Were Just Like Me . . . (What kind of church would this church be?)

Healthy Church . . . Start Here!

Light in a Dark Place

Order from:

    Carlton Coon Sr.
    4521 North Farm Road 165
    Springfield, MO 65803

Website: CarltonCoonSr.com

Personal Devotion

Table of Contents

Other Material by Carlton L. Coon Sr. 4
Overview of K.I.S.S. Keep It Simple Saints 9
Chapter 1 What is the Big Deal about Personal Devotion? 13
Chapter 2 Hindrances to Personal Devotion 15
Chapter 3 The Need for Quiet 19
Chapter 4 The Making of a Deeper Spiritual Life 25
Chapter 5 Personal Devotion Lights a Fire 27
Chapter 6 Models for Prayer 29
Chapter 7 God's Word and Personal Devotion 35
Chapter 8 Gain Full Benefit from Time in the Bible 39
Practical Guidelines for Your Personal Devotion 43

Personal Devotion

Personal Devotion

Overview of K.I.S.S.
Keep It Simple Saints

The acronym K.I.S.S. is likely familiar. K.I.S.S. has been used to express, "Keep it simple stupid!" Decision-makers often use the abbreviation K.I.S.S. The more complex a leader makes something, the "more stupid" the leader will eventually look. Effective leaders aim for simple.

The first "S" in K.I.S.S. means *simple*. A hammer is a *simple* machine. Using a hammer is uncomplicated.

Complications mar what should be easy. Doctors give lousy news by saying, "The surgery was simple, but there were some complications." Complex solutions are seldom understood, and even less often applied.

Keep it Simple Saints (K.I.S.S.) booklet**s** provide simple paths to understanding a Bible topic. The booklets include simple applications. In these booklets:

- The *K.I.S.S.* booklets are basic! An excellent foundational base is necessary to build a skyscraper.
- Suggestions are also given for sustaining your devotional life and winning the battle with the flesh, the world, and the devil.
- The book ends with a questionnaire that reviews the content.

Carlton L. Coon Sr.

Personal Devotion

Personal Devotion

Objective: *K.I.S.S. Quiet Time/Personal Devotion* introduces you to simple approaches and resources through which you can have a regular time with the Lord Jesus Christ.

Evaluating Your Devotion
(Score each question on a scale of 1-10.)
(1 = poor, 10 = excellent)

I realize the need to regularly spend time with God. _____

Over the past week, my personal devotion has been a _____

During personal devotion I can quiet my mind, spirit, and surroundings

_____

My personal devotion happens at the same time each day

_____

I take a consistent approach for my personal devotion _____

The Bible is part of my personal devotion _____

Books that guide my personal devotion are used _____

My prayer is clear. God knows what I am saying _____

Over two weeks, how often did you have personal devotion? (Put that number on the line.) _____

My personal devotion includes time to quietly listen to the Lord Jesus

_____

                                Total   _____

Scoring: 80-100 – Exceptional
                60-80 – Above Average
                30-60 – Average

Observation, rather than science, is the basis for the scoring.

The majority of Christians do not have a consistent personal devotion. You do not need to remain part of that group. If you use the resources in *K.I.S.S. – Personal Devotion,* you can spend quality time with the Lord Jesus.

Personal Devotion

Whatever your current score, with a bit of effort on your part, you can eventually have a healthy devotional life.

Personal Devotion

Chapter 1
What is the Big Deal about Personal Devotion?

You may be thinking, "Why should I take on the chore of establishing a new habit? I'm settled and content." By observing the spiritual lives of those who closely followed the Lord, we see the value of personal devotion.

Following a Good Precedent

Make a note about what and when each person did devotions.

Job 1:5

Psalms 5:3

Mark 1:35

"When" you spend time with God, is not as important as the fact of spending time with Him.

Genesis 24:63

Prayer was a consistent part of the life of Jesus Christ, Job, David, and Isaac. The first three prayed in the morning. Isaac's prayer, at least in this example, occurred in the evening.

Prayer is a Priority

The only thing Jesus' disciples ever asked Him to teach them was, "Lord, teach us to _____," (Luke 11:1).

1 Timothy 2:1: "I exhort therefore, that, _____ of all, supplications, _____, intercessions, and giving of thanks be made for all men."

Personal Devotion Includes the Bible

God's Word is "likened" to different things. Several times God's Word is spoken of as being "like" food. Spending time in the Bible is part of a proper

Personal Devotion

spiritual diet. Personal devotion will whet your appetite to know more about God through His Word.

Read the following verses and write down what food God's Word is "like."

1 Peter 2:2

Matthew 4:4

Hebrews 5:12

Jeremiah 15:26

Proper personal devotion seems to have these three characteristics:

- Consistency, whether the devotion happens morning, noon, or night.
- A conversation with the Lord Jesus Christ. This conversation is better known as *prayer*.
- Useful and meaningful time in God's Word.

Personal Devotion

Chapter 2
Hindrances to Personal Devotion

Have you had an experience where something important did not get followed through on? It happens often. You are familiar with such.

- You will reduce how much you eat.
- Saving money for a "rainy day" fund.
- Eliminating credit card debt.
- You will get fit by following an exercise plan.

You can add other things to the list. We all know of certain actions that need to happen. But these meaningful actions require change.

<u>Personal devotion needs to happen.</u> Most Christians understand this. We recognize the need to spend time with the Lord Jesus Christ. Yet, for many, a consistent personal devotion never happens.

What hinders us from practicing what we know is a benefit?

Prayerlessness

People who are unaware of the significance of prayer will never understand the value of daily time with God. A prayerless Christian is a powerless Christian. Prayer is not an optional exercise.

- Prayerlessness causes a loss of benefits you could claim. Ye _____ not, because ye _____ _____, (James 4:2).

- Prayerlessness keeps us from possessing the joy of the Lord. Ye have _____ nothing in my name, _____, and ye shall receive, that your joy may be full, (John 16:24).

- The prophet Samuel put the importance of prayer into perspective. God forbid that I should _____ against the LORD in ceasing to _____ for you, (1 Samuel 12:23).

Personal Devotion

Prayer is not an option for any Christian. Prayerlessness is sin. If the sin of prayerlessness is habitual in your life, repent and ask God to forgive you. Then become a man or woman of prayer.

No Specific Time

In physical exercise or the intent to study for an exam: *Sometimes* often ends up being *never.* The same is true with personal devotion. If there is not a specific time devoted to this practice, it won't happen.

I'm going to have personal devotion *"some time"* today works for only a few people.

Daniel was indicted for his consistency in prayer.

> **. . . he (Daniel) went into his house:**
>
> **and his windows being open in his chamber toward Jerusalem, he kneeled upon his knees three times a day, and _____ and gave _____ before his God, as he did _____,**
>
> **(Daniel 6:10).**

Daniel's daily habit of praying three times was not new. He had been practicing this for some time. Daniel had a specific time to pray.

The time for your devotion will be different than someone else. Each of us has a different life with different responsibilities. Don't feel bad if your approach to personal devotion does not mirror someone else.

<u>Consider the Morning</u>

More people have succeeded by having personal devotion in the morning than at any other time. The mornings are generally quieter. Most have the option of waking up thirty minutes earlier. As mentioned earlier, several Bible heroes prayed early in the day.

Morning devotion has a secondary benefit. Your entire day will be flavored with having started it in fellowship with the Lord Jesus Christ. Things you

Personal Devotion

prayed about, read in the Bible, or heard from God will come back to you during the day.

When do you think will be your best time for personal devotion? Choose three. You may experience times when your first choice will not work. By planning ahead, you will already have a second choice in mind.

1.

2.

3.

Lack of a Specific Place

Grabbing any convenient spot to pray will make it hard to maintain personal devotion. One of my mentors had a particular rocking chair in which he would sit and pray. It was his specific place of prayer. Several acquaintances have established a "closet" of prayer. The closet includes an altar at which they can kneel.

Daniel had a specific place He prayed before an open window looking toward Jerusalem. It was Daniel's place for prayer.

Jesus had a place He often used for prayer. Jesus was "wont (to go) to the Mount of Olives," (Luke 22:39). The Garden of Gethsemane is on the Mount of Olives. Jesus probably had several places of prayer, but the Garden of Gethsemane on the Mount of Olives was one of them.

It need not be that prayer is the only thing that happens in your specific place. But part of its identity, at least in your mind, should be your place of prayer. It is best if your particular site is relatively uncluttered and without a constant flow of traffic.

Where do you think the best locations would be for your specific place of prayer?

1.

2.

3.

Personal Devotion

No Devotional Plan

For a person to say, "I'm going to pray," is commendable. It is a great start. However, to be successful in any of the disciplines mentioned in the first paragraph, there must be a plan.

- To change your diet, you will need a plan.
- Becoming fit requires a fitness plan.
- Competent students develop a study plan.

Few meaningful things happen without a plan. A section of this booklet will explore some different strategies to consider. If you feel that this help is needed NOW, find that section of the book. Read about the devotional plans and select a devotional plan with which to start.

Your Personal Commitment

I will commit to a time of personal devotion. It will happen on

_____ (days of the week) at _____ (time) in

_____ (place). I will start this journey on _____

(date). If these days, this time, or place do not work for me, I will try alternatives.

Personal Devotion

Chapter 3
The Need for Quiet

Desiring a quiet time with God comes when you realize how tumultuous life is. Your devotion will be better if you do not have a lot of noise or chaos around you. In your "place" for devotion, turn off the radio and television. Put your phone on silent. Quiet the "alerts" that come to your electronic devices.

Remove distractions and focus on the Lord Jesus Christ.

Psalm 46:10: "Be _____, and know that I am God."

Israel was at war at the time of the writing of Psalm 46. The Psalm challenged the people to quietness during a time of turbulence.

Our Noisy World

We live in a noisy world. While writing this, I was in Vancouver, alone in a hotel room. But it wasn't quiet:

> The door across the hall just closed.
> My room's air conditioning unit was making an odd noise.
> A diesel truck started in the parking lot.
> There was the clatter of breaking glass from a pub down the way.
> A tugboat on the Fraser River just sounded its horn.
> The clack of my fingers on the computer keys was noisy.
> The air conditioner compressor kicked on.
> A pigeon squawked outside my window.
> The refrigerator was humming.
> An e-mail provider heralded, "You've Got Mail!"

Is it quiet where you are reading? For thirty seconds, stop reading. List every sound you hear:

Personal Devotion

As you think about a typical day, you will likely realize how rare it is to be "still" to know that He is God. Quiet is at a premium. "Silent" vacations are a big marketing promotion for some resorts. Hotel chains offer quiet floors. Noise-canceling headphones sell at a premium, and earplugs serve to hush the outside world.[1]

Earth is a noisy place!

But your God is not particularly noisy.

Many corporate executives say they do their best work on an airplane. Why? At least in part because an attendant says, "The door is now closed. Please turn your cell phones to airplane mode."

Your best personal devotion will most often happen in a quiet place.

Validate the Quiet

Perhaps you have not yet seen the value of the quiet. When we are in constant noise we do not see the value of quiet. People of significance and creativity help give credence to the need for quiet.

> Silence is the element in which great things fashion themselves.
> Scottish Philosopher Thomas Carlyle

> The great things are quiet.
> You never hear the sun, nor the dew, nor the light,
> but they dominate all of life.
> Powerful things happen in silence.
> Author/Evangelist S.D. Gordon

> Quiet minds cannot be perplexed or frightened,
> but go on in fortune or misfortune at their own private pace,
> like a clock during a thunderstorm.
> Author Robert Louis Stevenson

---

[1] Paskin, Janet in *Ode*, July/August 2008; as cited in *Discipleship Journal* p. 14, November/December 2008.

Personal Devotion

In spite of much evidence we struggle to find quiet. Does our relatively quiet God look aghast at how noisy it is when we try to talk to Him?

The answer is to unplug. Silence everything, with perhaps the exception of soft non-intrusive music. You and Jesus, meeting at "your favorite place."

Mental and Spiritual Disquiet

Disquiet - goes beyond "noise." Disquiet is a lack of peace or rest. Do you feel intruded on? The tension you feel when intrusions come is an indication of disquiet.

Soul-numbing exhaustion sets in if you are overly accessible; activities that renew the soul, spirit, mind, and body are cancelled. Things like taking a walk, birdwatching, contemplating a paragraph in the Bible, reading some of Kahlil Gibran's poems, enjoying a Saturday morning of yard sales, or picking up a basketball game – are interrupted to multi-task.

Selah is a word found in the Psalms. It means, "Pause and consider this." If we do not 'pause,' neither can we, 'consider this!'

Do you have "availability addiction?"[2] Has pride lured you into believing the world cannot continue without your direct involvement? Texting, Twittering, Instagram, Facebook, Linked-in, responding to e-mail or talking on the phone leave you inaccessible to Jesus.

In 1949, the *Saturday Evening Post* included a memorable poem titled, "The Mad Atom."

> This is the age
> Of the half-read page.
> And the quick hash
> And the mad dash.
> The bright night
> With the nerves tight.
> The plane hop
> With the brief stop.

---

[2] P. 34, Barton, Ruth Haley. *Discipleship Journal*, September/October 2005.

Personal Devotion

> The lamp tan
> In a short span.
> The Big Shot
> In a good spot.
> And the brain strain
> The heart pain.
> And the cat naps
> Till the spring snaps --
> And the fun's done!

Even with the addition of thousands of labor-saving devices, the "dash" is "madder" than ever. Do you notice that during devotion, you remember the groceries you need or a phone call you must return? It is hard to get off the mental treadmill.

Write down three or four sentences that describe your "mad dash." Think about this exercise. It is easy to be oblivious to how much your life is out-of-control.

-
-
-
-

Practical Tip: Keep a notepad nearby. Use it to jot down any chores, tasks, or projects you think of while you are having your quiet time or personal devotion. Physically writing these down moves them out of your mind. You can now refocus on your time with God. At the same time, you needn't fret about the thought getting away from you.

It is unfortunate when inner disquiet becomes normal. Inner restlessness is not the will of God. So, where does this pace originate?

Personal Devotion

The devil wants you to be in a hurry and rush,
go pell mell and not wait for anything,
whereas <u>Jesus is always quiet</u>, and He is <u>always calm</u>
and <u>always takes His time</u>.
20th Century Holiness Evangelist
G.D. Watson

A desk placard on one pastor's desk reads:

"When you are faced with a busy day,
save precious time –
skip your devotions."
Satan

The pivotal word in Satan's suggestion is the word *time*. The idea conveys that devotion is less important than your workout, washing the car or a myriad of "other things" that make up a busy day.

How time gets used is in your hands. Personal devotion requires scheduling and attention.

List five activities that could have the potential to make your life such a rush that you have no time for personal devotion.

    1.

    2.

    3.

    4.

    5.

List three issues that have the potential to become a mental distraction.

    1.

    2.

    3.

Personal Devotion

Recognizing your potential challenges to being still can help you develop a personal strategy to overcome them.

Personal Devotion
Chapter 4
The Making of a Deeper Spiritual Life

It is your responsibility to determine the depth of your life.
God will determine the breadth of your life.

Personal devotion is the gateway to a deeper spiritual life. But, it won't be sudden. Spiritual growth is not instant oatmeal. We are impatient.

- I want God, and I want Him now!
- I want spiritual maturity, and I want it now!

Such expectations are unrealistic. When you start a fitness regimen, you accept the fact that results take time. The same principle applies to things of God.

Your quiet encounters with God through personal devotion allow you to connect with Him regularly. These encounters are not always based on your pastor's sermon or Bible Study.

If a man has no private encounters with the Lord Jesus, is that man dishonest when he talks of Jesus' importance to him? The God you discover at the quiet center of your personal devotional life will bring depth to your life.

Be Realistic

Personal devotion will not make you suddenly superbly spiritual. Generally, God's work in us is slow and steady. Your everyday act of investing in personal devotion will affect the shape of your decisions. These moments with Him mold us into His desire.

On many seashores, trees are in bizarre shapes. The shapes are not the result of hurricane-force winds. More often, these unusual shapes are the result of the steady breeze. The constant wind shapes those trees.

What daily wind is shaping your life?

Personal devotion will be a different wind. The steady influence will shape your life. Through a gradual process, your thoughts, ambitions, desires, and behavior will change.

Personal Devotion

In regard to personal growth the Lord Jesus is not into quick fixes. In Genesis 28, Jacob dreamed of a ladder set on the earth. The top reached to heaven. There were angels on the ladder.

Angels on a ladder seems to be an unnatural thing. In the popular imagination, we envision angels having wings. Wings or not, the angels on Jacob's ladder did not fly. They ascended from one step to another.

In a similar your personal devotion will not suddenly take you to great heights with God. Instead, envision yourself climbing a ladder, one rung at a time, each step moving you upward.[3]

---

[3] P 70 Willard, Dallas. The Spirit of the Disciplines. HarperOne, 1999.

Personal Devotion

Chapter 5
Personal Devotion Lights a Fire

Life can dampen your spiritual enthusiasm. Disappointments are a bit like rain on a campfire. These can take away your energy for the things of God. Carrying out your commitment to personal devotion will help keep your spiritual fire burning.

Soon after Jesus' resurrection from the dead, two of His followers were walking to the village of Emmaus. They discussed the things that had happened in Jerusalem. Jesus drew near, but they did not recognize Him. He asked the two, "Why are you sad?" The two men told Him of the crucifixion and the rumors of the Lord being alive.

Jesus took the scripture and explained these events to them. Still, the two men did not know who Jesus was. Upon arriving in Emmaus, the travelers invited Jesus to stay with them. At dinner, Jesus took bread, blessed it, and gave it to them. Then, they knew Him. They said one to another:

Did not our heart _____ within us, while he talked with us by the

way, and while he opened to us the _____? (Luke 24:32)

Personal devotion will keep your spiritual fire alive. Look again at Luke 24:13-32. Two components determined the outcome for these two men. These same elements are vital to you.

- First, there was a conversation between the men and Jesus. Your personal devotion will include prayer, a conversation between you and the Lord Jesus Christ.
- Second, the scripture was a priority. God's Word will also be a significant part of your personal devotion. You have a benefit the two men traveling to Emmaus did not have. Not only do you have access to Moses and all the prophets, but also to all of the New Testament.

Your devotion will keep a fire going in your spiritual life. Depression, despair, and disappointment will come. Sickness and grief may knock at your door. In

Personal Devotion

such times, continue to walk and talk with Jesus. Keep on spending time with the scripture.

Personal Devotion
Chapter 6
Models for Prayer

One danger to personal devotion is in it becoming a technique to be pursued. Having a pattern through which you approach personal devotion is beneficial. But the model should not become the end-all.

Personal devotion is more than checking off several boxes. Personal devotion should not be something you do. It is to be something you live. The wrong attitude says, "I've done my two paragraphs of Bible study for today," or, "I've done my prayer journal . . . so now I'm done with God for the day." Our "devotion" to God continues after we have quietly spent time with Him.

Below, three models for prayer are suggested. These are places to start. Plan to go beyond them. None of the suggested options may work for you. Continue seeking until you find a pattern that works. Use the model as a start, and then grow.

Pray the Lord's Prayer

In Matthew 6:9-13, Jesus provided a model for prayer. His prayer was not something to simply repeat. Instead, it was an approach. The Lord's prayer is a beautiful pattern.

1. Quiet your mind. Focus your attention on the Father. Jesus did this in the first two phrases of His model: "Our Father, which art in heaven, hallowed be thy name." *Hallowed* means "to be kept holy" or "to be kept set apart."
2. Appeal for His kingdom to come. The kingdom of God brings spiritual renewal and refreshing. The coming of the kingdom of God to your community will result in revival.
3. Release yourself to His will. Jesus' model said, "Thy will be done in earth as it is in heaven." How is God's will done in heaven? In heaven, God's will is final! During this part of the prayer, you will be surrendering to His purpose for you during the day.

Personal Devotion

4. Ask for the Lord's help with your daily needs. Jesus put it this way, "Give us this day our daily bread." Your God knows you have needs. Ask for His aid.
5. Seek forgiveness for your sin, even as you realize you must forgive others.
6. Ask God to keep you from temptation and to deliver from evil.
7. Declare His Kingdom authority and power overall in your life and all that is around you.
8. End with "Amen." Amen is a word of affirmation. An amen is you saying, "So be it, God."

Praying Through the Tabernacle

The Tabernacle in the Wilderness was the first place where God consistently met His people. When praying through the Tabernacle, you use each piece of furniture to prompt well-rounded prayer.

If interested in the exact layout of the Tabernacle, you can easily find a portrayal online. "Praying Through the Tabernacle" includes the following.

1. The gate opening into the Tabernacle - Thanksgiving
2. The courtyard – Praise God for what He has done!
3. The Brazen Altar - Confession
4. The Brazen Laver – Cleansing
5. The Table of Shewbread - Petition
6. The Golden Candlestick – Ministering to the Lord
7. The Altar of Incense – Intercession
8. Holy of Holies – This is the inner sanctuary of the presence of God. The Holy of Holies calls me to worship God because of who He is.

These eight steps need to be Biblically validated.

#1 ***The Gate*** – Thanksgiving! "Enter into His gates with _____," (Psalm 100:4). Begin with thanks for what the Lord Jesus Christ has already done for you.

Personal Devotion

#2 *The Courtyard* - The place of praise. ... "and into His courts with _____," (Psalm 100:4).

#3 *The Brazen Altar* - A place for confession. Sacrifice was made at the Brazen Altar. Jesus is your "once and for all time, sacrifice." You do not pay the price for your sin. The price has already paid. At the altar, you confess.

#4 *The Brass Laver* - The place of cleansing. In speaking of the church, Ephesians says, "That he might sanctify and _____ it by the washing of water by the _____, (Ephesians 5:26). God's Word cleans us up. During this step, you would spend time in the Bible.

#5 *The Table of Shewbread* - Here, we make our appeals to God. The bread on the Table of Shewbread was eventually food for priests. God was providing for those who served Him. In Matthew 6:11, you are taught to pray, "_____ us this day our daily bread."

#6 *The Golden Candlestick* - This is where we prepare to do ministry. The Golden Candlestick provided the only illumination in the Tabernacle. Light and "good works" come together in Matthew 5:16: "Let your _____ so shine before men, that they may see your _____ _____, and glorify your Father which is in heaven."

#7 *The Altar of Incense* - The place of intercession. In Revelation 8, the Altar of Incense speaks of intercession. Intercession involves praying for others.

#8 *The Holy of Holies* - This is where the Ark of the Covenant sat. The Ark of the Covenant reminds us of God's covenant with us. Because the mercy seat was atop the Ark, it serves to remind of God's mercy toward us. Here was

Personal Devotion

where the glory of God would meet with man. God's glory always prompts worship.

God R.E.A.C.T.S Prayer

God hears and responds to prayer. Knowing and expecting Him to react to our relationship and requests offers another pattern for devotion. God R.E.A.C.T.S.!

R = *Reflection*
E = *Exaltation*
A = *Admitting your need for Him*
C = *Confession of sin*
T = *Thanksgiving*
S = *Supplication*

This pattern works for verbal prayer or prayer journaling. If you journal, the daily devotion would take these steps.

<u>Reflection</u> – Think about what happened in your life yesterday. If it has been several days since your last personal devotion, think about the entire time. Write down some of the key happenings. The goal is a time of introspection. Introspection slows the mind.

<u>Exaltation</u> – How great is our God? How great is His name? In exaltation, celebrate some single attribute of God. To accomplish this, you will need devotional books focusing on nothing but exalting Him.

<u>Admission</u> – "I need thee, oh I need thee, every hour I need thee . . ." Admit your dependence on Him. Reject pride, arrogance, and human talent as the strength of life. Be specific in the areas where you need Jesus to intervene.

<u>Confession</u> – We all fail. There are times we miss the mark. Human failure can be sordid. "If we _____ our sins, he is faithful and just to _____ us our sins," (1 John 1:9).

Personal Devotion

Thanksgiving – In reflection or through the moments of prayer, you will recall answers God has provided. Be thankful for His goodness to you.

Supplication – Supplication is making a request or interceding. .Philippians 4:6: "Be careful for nothing but in every thing by prayer and _____ with thanksgiving let your _____ be made known unto God." The verse is telling you not to overload with worry. Instead, take your cares to God.

Personal Devotion

Personal Devotion

Chapter 7

God's Word and Personal Devotion

The Bible is vital in personal devotion. Material designed to assist in personal devotion can be a blessing or a curse. If the book you use does not force you to think about the scripture, then it has failed in its purpose.

God highly values His Word. He has magnified his _____ above His

_____. (Psalms 138:2)

It is not wrong to use devotionals, but be sure to select devotional material that does not think for you. God's Word is exalted; it is not dependent on what anyone else says about His Word.

As is the case for prayer, there are many ways to use the Bible in personal devotion. Whatever approach you use, do the following.

Pray for Understanding

God can help you discover beneficial things in His Word. The Holy Ghost is a teacher, (John 14:26).

Paul said he spoke of things "which the Holy Ghost _____,

comparing spiritual things with _____," (1 Corinthians 2:13).

The Bible itself gives the most significant commentary about God's Word.

Plan

It is not best to just open your Bible each day and read the chapter you happen to notice. Reading the Bible becomes effective by having a plan. Consider the following.

<u>A Paragraph each Day</u>

Your Bible has chapters and verses. Many Bibles include paragraph markings. All three of the divisions – chapter, verse, and paragraph were imposed on the

Personal Devotion

text centuries after the Bible was written. Considering a single paragraph allows you to take hold of the text mentally. You may learn more considering a paragraph than by reading five chapters.

In considering the paragraph, think about the following:

1. Who was writing?
2. To whom was it written?
3. What was the message to the original reader?
4. How is this relevant to me?
5. What questions does this paragraph suggest?

You will increase the impact of your time with the Bible if you write down the answers to these five questions, as well as any other thoughts that occur.

A paragraph a day will not get you through the Bible in a year. However, at the end of working your way through the Bible, you will likely know far more than if you had read the Bible through five times.

<u>Examine a Topic</u>

A topical study must be done correctly. For accurate understanding, any verse must be considered in its natural context. Understanding what is being said about a topic will usually requires considering several verses. In some instances, an entire chapter or book may bear on the matter. Using scripture out of context results in foolish ideas.

The topical study is worth trying. There are online guides for studying topics. These guides may be useful, but do not let the verse or two they provide be all you read. Look on either side of the verse cited. Further, seek other information on the topic.

Nave's Topical Bible is now online and provides much content on many topics. The *Thompson Chain Reference Bible* has been used for decades to make a thorough study of a topic. While using these resources are others like them, read the verses surrounding the one the resource suggests.

Personal Devotion

<u>Learn about a Bible Character</u>

It can also be beneficial to read about one individual in the Bible. Perhaps you are interested in David, the man after God's own heart. In such a study, you would do the following.

1. Find all portions of scripture mentioning David. You can get a list of these from a concordance. Online concordances are readily available. If you prefer a physical book – *Cruden's Concordance* and *Strong's Exhaustive Concordance* are standards.
2. Seek the earliest reference to David. Read what the Bible says about that event.
3. You will progressively work your way through the passages. In some instances, a different book of history will cover the same ground. In such cases, read carefully. There are two different accounts for a reason.

You will again benefit from making notes. Consider the following questions in each section having to do with the character:

1. What did I learn about the Bible character in this passage?
2. What did I learn about God in the passage of scripture?

This sort of study can become entrancing, causing a desire to learn more.

These are only a few options to consider. There are many other approaches for the Bible to be part of your devotion.

Personal Devotion

Personal Devotion
Chapter 8
Gain Full Benefit from Time in the Bible

This chapter will offer assorted suggestions for improving your use of the Bible.

Practical Insight

Use a physical Bible for reading and study. The Bible is on my phone, iPad, and computer. For free, the Bible can be listened to or read in several different translations. Computer software and apps make the Bible more accessible, but for compiling information and keeping notes in the margin, a physical Bible wins.

With a physical Bible, you can highlight, underline, and write notes in the margin. Bible Study apps do offer these benefits. What apps cannot provide is the opportunity to thumb through your Bible until your eye falls on a portion of scripture that benefitted you in the past. When you read your margin notes, the part of scripture comes alive again.

Caveat: If you are of the digital generation and have the ability to use an app like *Evernote* or some Bible application in a way that allows you to highlight, make notes that pop back up when you read, etc. use what works best for you. Just be sure you "use it hard."

Memorize the books of the Bible Having the books memorized allows you to move about your Bible more easily. Even with easy access to the Bible via apps knowing the order of the books helps put arrange how different sections it together.

If you have not spent much time in the Bible, it may seem foreign. Keep reading. The Bible will become more comfortable as your understanding increases.

Knowing the order of the books of the Bible will be a help. Start by memorizing the 27 books of the New Testament, then learn the 39 books of the Old Testament.

Personal Devotion

Pursue God's Wisdom

The Wisdom of God is in Proverbs. Consider reading a chapter of Proverbs each day. On the 1st day of each month, read chapter 1, on the second day, read chapter 2, and so on through the month. At the start of the next month, go back to chapter 1.

The book of Proverbs provides practical instructions for daily life. It gives guidance on everything from lending money to getting along with your spouse. What you gain from Proverbs is not the advice of a therapist. Instead, it is the wisdom of God.

Practial Tip: Add the pursuit of God's wisdom by reading the book of Proverbs to whatever other methods you use. You will never go wrong following the wisdom of God.

Personalize Your Bible

A worn-out Bible usually belongs to someone not worn out. Part of the wear on a Bible is underling and highlighting verses that speak to you. Mark your Bible in a way that benefits you.

Information learned about a character, or two verses that suddenly connect is noted in the margin of my study Bible. Such margin notes, and being assertive while preaching have resulted in me wearing out several *Scofield Study Bibles* and *Thompson Chain Reference* Bibles.

My margin notes help make the text alive to me. Often when a particular section is read there is a new note to add. A Bible with extra-wide margins is useful for devotional purposes, but is not what you would want to take to work. It is a large book.

Seek Application

Your time in the Bible is not just to gain information. God's Word is the sword of the Spirit. The Bible is full of applications.

As you read, contemplate, or examine a text, ask yourself, "What am I to do about this?" Reading the Bible is intended to produce positive change in your life. Some examples:

Personal Devotion

- How you treat others will likely improve.
- You may more closely filter what you read, watch, and that to which you listen.
- You may become more gracious and fair to your employees.
- As a laborer, you may realize that not working hard through the entire day is actually stealing from your employer.

Part of your devotion should include asking God to help you apply what you learn.

Reading the Bible is not just about gaining information. Reading the Bible is done for personal transformation.

Personal Devotion

Personal Devotion

Practical Guidelines for Your Personal Devotion

This chapter is a summation of the things discussed earlier. These are bullet points to help you focus on spending quality time with God:

- ✓ Block out 15-30 minutes of each day for personal devotion! Do not let anything else creep in or replace the time. Treat your appointment with God as you would a meeting with a powerful government official.
- ✓ Use one of the models of prayer presented earlier or some other pattern you have discovered. Quieten your setting by turning off things that produce noise. Have a notebook handy on which to write tasks that come to mind.
- ✓ Quiet your mind and spirit before beginning your time with God.
- ✓ When you transition to your time with God's Word, ask God to <u>say something</u> to you through the Bible. Do not let your time with God be one-way. Allow Him to speak to you through the Bible and through the Holy Ghost.
- ✓ As you read the portion of scripture, you are focusing on keeping several questions in mind:
    - ❏ Who is speaking or writing?
    - ❏ To whom are they speaking or writing?
    - ❏ What was the issue at hand in this passage of scripture?
    - ❏ What was God saying to the participants?
    - ❏ How is this relevant to my life? What is God saying to me?
    - ❏ How do I apply this to my everyday life?

Pay attention to the commands, the warnings, the promises, and the good and bad examples that you come across.

Millions of people throughout history have practiced personal devotion. You can be successful as well.

Personal Devotion

Review K.I.S.S. – Personal Devotion

1. What are two things that have the potential of getting in the way of practicing personal devotion?

   -
   -

2. Quiet and stillness can be difficult to find. Yet in a time of conflict the Lord told Israel to be _____ and know that I am _____. How will you find quiet and stillness?

   -

3. What are some of the benefits of doing personal devotion early in the day?

   -
   -

4. Jesus' instruction in prayer included, "Give us this day our daily bread." What can this portion of prayer prompt us to do during our personal devotion?

   -
   -

5. Effective sustained personal devotion usually requires having a specific t_____ and a certain p_____. How did the prophet Daniel accomplish these two things?

   -

6. If a person enters the Holy of Holies during personal devotion, what are they likely to be doing?

   -

Personal Devotion

7. When you read a portion of the scripture as part of your personal devotion, what are two of the questions you should always ask regarding the text?

   -
   -

8. The book of _____ is the wisdom of God.

9. Effective personal devotion not only involves speaking to God but also _____ to Him. What are the two primary means God uses to speak to us?

   -
   -

10. Learning more from the Bible usually includes having a pattern for systematic study and making n_____.

May God's blessing be on you in your journey of personal growth with the Lord Jesus Christ. There are no quick paths to spiritual maturity, but the available path to spiritual maturity is an easy walk if you follow it. Spend time with Him. Just you and Him. Jesus will become more precious to you. You will become wiser in life and represent Him better.

Carlton L. Coon Sr.

Made in the USA
Middletown, DE
10 May 2024

53937278R00027